THE
RUGBY
UNION
QUIZ BOOK

THE RUGBY UNION QUIZ BOOK

MATTHEW JONES

y Lolfa

First impression: 2015
© Matthew Jones & Y Lolfa Cyf., 2015

Cover design: Y Lolfa

ISBN: 978 1 78461 117 0

Published and printed in Wales
on paper from well-maintained forests by
Y Lolfa Cyf., Talybont, Ceredigion SY24 5HE
e-mail ylolfa@ylolfa.com
website www.ylolfa.com
tel 01970 832 304
fax 832 782

Introduction

The game of rugby union has developed significantly since its origins on the playing fields of Rugby School, where in 1823 William Webb Ellis picked the ball up during a game of football and ran with it. Since then we have seen rugby clubs becoming integral parts of their communities, and a thirst for the international game sees matches broadcast across the globe.

The rugby union fan has certainly been entertained over the decades with moments of scintillating skill, flair and bravery. For those who adore nothing better than a fifty-yard run finished off by a dramatic try, images of a moment of magic from a Serge Blanco, David Campese, Jeff Wilson or Gerald Davies probably resonates well in the memory. Others enjoy nothing more than a tough scrum with the pure force, technical ability and aggression of eight against eight deciding supremacy.

The game has been laden with international superstars such as Jonah Lomu, Jonny Wilkinson, Gareth Edwards, Hugo Porta and Brian O'Driscoll. This list is far from exclusive and could easily go on for several paragraphs if not pages.

There are certain moments in life that you'll never forget, and for a hardened fan of the oval ball, a first rugby match must sit right up there, whether at a local pitch or in one of the great sporting amphitheatres of the world such as Eden Park, Thomond Park or Twickenham.

This book is an opportunity for you to test your knowledge of the fantastic game. The questions are a mixture, some hard, others easier. There's something in here for every type of supporter. Hope you enjoy...

Matthew Jones
July 2015

Round 1

1. **Gareth Edwards, Sid Going and Ken Catchpole appeared in over 100 international matches between them. Which position would you associate with these players?**

    a) Scrum-half
    b) Outside-half
    c) Wing

2. **Ireland lost 23–16 to Wales in the 2015 Six Nations championship. Who won his 100th Irish cap on the day?**

    a) Rory Best
    b) Jamie Heaslip
    c) Paul O'Connell

3. **Who made his England debut at the age of 30 against Australia in 1988?**

    a) Jeff Probyn
    b) Paul Ackford
    c) Wade Dooley

4. **South Africa won a record 17 consecutive matches from 1997 to 1998. Who was their captain during this run?**

    a) Gary Teichmann
    b) Joost van der Westhuizen
    c) Mark Andrews

5. Who scored a try on his New Zealand debut at Dunedin's Carisbrook Stadium against Scotland in 1990, then scored a try on his 50th appearance against the same opposition, at the same stadium and nearly at the same spot six years later?

   a) Frank Bunce
   b) Olo Brown
   c) Ian Jones

6. Who was the only Scottish international to play for the Barbarians in their famous 23–11 victory over New Zealand in 1973?

   a) Peter Brown
   b) Gordon Brown
   c) Sandy Carmichael

7. Which side won the French championship five times during the 1990s?

   a) Toulouse
   b) Brive
   c) Biarritz

8. Which player, born in Zambia, retired from international rugby in 2007 as the world's most capped player with 139 Tests under his belt?

9. Who scored 228 points in 26 British and Irish Lions matches during the 1974 tour of South Africa and the 1977 tour of New Zealand?

10. In 2012, which New Zealand international became the first player to win a World Cup, Super Rugby title and a European Cup?

Round 2

1. **In which country did the Currie Cup become an annual competition in 1968?**
    a) South Africa
    b) Italy
    c) Argentina

2. **Which hooker from the 1980s and 1990s was known as 'The Pit-bull'?**
    a) Kevin Phillips
    b) Sean Fitzpatrick
    c) Brian Moore

3. **During the 1995 Rugby World Cup, who became the first All Black to score six tries in a Test match?**
    a) Jeff Wilson
    b) Jonah Lomu
    c) Marc Ellis

4. **Which versatile back became the youngest Wallaby since Brian Ford in 1957 when he made his debut in 2008 against Italy?**
    a) Digby Ioane
    b) Pat McCabe
    c) James O'Connor

5. Hollywood actor, Matt Damon, starred in the 2009 Clint Eastwood directed film *Invictus*. Which former Springbok did he depict in the film?

   a) Joel Stransky
   b) Francois Pienaar
   c) André Joubert

6. Scotland beat Romania 12–6 in 1981. In the game Andy Irvine scored his 209th international point to set a new world record. Whose record did he overtake?

   a) Don Clarke
   b) Barry John
   c) Tom Kiernan

7. Who scored a brace of tries as Wales defeated France by a record score of 21–0 at Cardiff in 1950?

   a) Ken Jones
   b) Jack Matthews
   c) Gerwyn Williams

8. Which Irishman's 29-cap international career spanned over 15 years with a first cap in 1955 and the last coming in 1970?

9. Who was England team manager for 49 matches from January 1988 until March 1994?

10. Which country in 2013 recorded their first back-to-back Six Nations wins since 2001?

Round 3

1. **What's the colour of Italy's home shirt?**
   - a) White
   - b) Red
   - c) Blue

2. **Which country won four Six Nations championships in a ten-year period from 2005?**
   - a) France
   - b) Wales
   - c) Ireland

3. **Which 33-year-old former scrum-half became France coach in 1981?**
   - a) Jacques Fouroux
   - b) Max Barrau
   - c) Gérard Sutra

4. **Reginald Birkett, Charles Wilson and John Sutcliffe have what in common?**
   - a) Won England caps in rugby union and football
   - b) Earned international caps for the British and Irish Lions before playing for England
   - c) Played for England while serving in the army

5. **Lock Cristian Petre set a 92-cap national record in 2012. Which country did he represent?**
   - a) Russia
   - b) France
   - c) Romania

6. **Ponsonby Rugby Club was founded in 1874. In which New Zealand city is the club based?**

    a) Wellington
    b) Auckland
    c) Palmerston North

7. **Who did Canada defeat 18–16 in June 1994?**

    a) France
    b) England
    c) New Zealand

8. **Whose 24-try international world record stood from 1933 until eclipsed by David Campese in 1987?**

9. **New Zealand outside-half Frano Botica joined which Welsh club side in 1996?**

10. **England defeated Wales 25–6 at Cardiff on 19 January 1991. Who successfully kicked seven penalties in the match to set a new national record?**

Round 4

1. **For which country did Robert Howley earn 59 caps from 1996 until 2002?**
    - a) Scotland
    - b) Australia
    - c) Wales

2. **Speaking before the first British and Irish Lions Test against South Africa in 1997, who said 'To win for the Lions in a Test match is the ultimate. The opposition don't rate you. They don't respect you. The only way to be rated is to stick one up them'?**
    - a) Jim Telfer
    - b) Martin Johnson
    - c) Ieuan Evans

3. **Who made 45 consecutive appearances for France from 1982 to 1987?**
    - a) Serge Blanco
    - b) Philippe Sella
    - c) Pierre Berbizier

4. **Who did Italy defeat 19–22 away from home in the 2015 Six Nations championship?**
    - a) Ireland
    - b) Wales
    - c) Scotland

5. **Who was the top points' scorer at the 1999 Rugby World Cup?**
    a) Gonzalo Quesada
    b) Neil Jenkins
    c) Matthew Burke

6. **Which Irish province defeated Australia for a third time with a 22–19 victory in 1992?**
    a) Ulster
    b) Munster
    c) Leinster

7. **Who became the fourth Englishman to lead his country on his Test debut when he appeared against Australia in 1984?**
    a) Nigel Melville
    b) Richard Hill
    c) Jon Hall

8. **During the 1980s, which pair of brothers became the first twins to play together for New Zealand?**

9. **Heyneke Meyer was named head coach of which country in 2012?**

10. **Which future British and Irish Lion left the union game in 1988 by transferring from Sale to Leeds in rugby league for £80,000?**

Round 5

1. **Who captained Australia to their 1991 Rugby World Cup title?**

    a) Nick Farr-Jones

    b) David Campese

    c) Rod McCall

2. **How many caps in total were won by Alain Penaud (1992–2000), Peter Clohessy (1993–2002) and Paul Thorburn (1985–1991)?**

    a) 123

    b) 169

    c) 191

3. **Which New Zealand back-row forward of the 1980s was known as 'Buck'?**

    a) Mark Shaw

    b) Andy Earl

    c) Wayne Shelford

4. **Which club was the first to provide 100 internationals for the Scotland national side?**

    a) Edinburgh Wanderers

    b) Hawick

    c) London Scottish

5. **'Bloodgate' was an incident on 12 April 2009 when a Harlequins player used a blood capsule to fake an injury in a game Leinster won 6–5. Who was the player who took the capsule?**

      a) Nick Evans

      b) Tom Williams

      c) Chris Robshaw

6. **Who captained Canada to a 26–23 victory over Scotland in June 2002?**

      a) Al Charron

      b) Rod Snow

      c) Jon Thiel

7. **Which back-row forward was Welsh player of the year in both 1974 and 1978?**

      a) Derek Quinnell

      b) Terry Cobner

      c) Dai Morris

8. **Selkirk outside-half John Rutherford made 42 Scotland international appearances. He partnered the same scrum-half on 35 of these occasions. Who was the scrum-half?**

9. **Who started the 1995 Rugby World Cup final for South Africa at full-back with a broken hand?**

10. **England internationals Ray Longland, Gary Pearce and David Powell played for a combined total of 55 years for the same club. Which club was this?**

Round 6

1. **Barry John, Paul McLean and Craig Chalmers played rugby at which position?**
   a) Wing
   b) Outside-half
   c) Flanker

2. **Which ground hosted the first Rugby World Cup final in 1987?**
   a) Eden Park, Auckland
   b) Lancaster Park, Christchurch
   c) Athletic Park, Wellington

3. **In which year did London Scottish's Lindsay Renwick, Neath's Phil Pugh and Harlequins' Andy Mullins win their only international cap?**
   a) 1985
   b) 1987
   c) 1989

4. **Which New Zealand prop received a nine-month ban for eye gouging fellow All Black Greg Cooper in the 1992 national championship final?**
   a) Richard Loe
   b) Steve McDowell
   c) Kevin Boroevich

5. **Who made the most appearances (23 games) on the 1966 British and Irish Lions tour of Australia and New Zealand?**

    a) Alun Pask
    b) Delme Thomas
    c) Dewi Bebb

6. **France defeated Scotland 15–8 in the 2015 Six Nations. Who scored all of France's points in his first tournament start?**

    a) Rory Kockott
    b) Rémi Talès
    c) Camille Lopez

7. **England defeated Wales 7–3 at Twickenham in 1923. Who set a record for England's fastest try, touching down ten seconds into the match?**

    a) Geoffrey Conway
    b) Leo Price
    c) Cyril Lowe

8. **Who kicked all 21 points in Argentina's 1985 draw against New Zealand?**

9. **Which Irishman was named International Rugby Board player of the year in 2001?**

10. **South Africa defeated Ireland 23–15 in May 1981. Who became the first black player to start a Test for the Springboks in this match?**

Round 7

1. **Which country carries the emblem of a silver fern as its badge on its jerseys?**
   - a) Tonga
   - b) USA
   - c) New Zealand

2. **The Melrose Cup is awarded to the winner of which tournament?**
   - a) Rugby World Cup Sevens
   - b) Six Nations Championship
   - c) The Rugby Championship

3. **Which country's team arrived in the United Kingdom for their 1939 tour only to find out that the Second World War had broken out and had to return without putting on their boots?**
   - a) New Zealand
   - b) Australia
   - c) South Africa

4. **Who scored 22 tries in 23 matches during the British and Irish Lions' 1959 tour of Australia and New Zealand?**
   - a) Terry Davies
   - b) Peter Jackson
   - c) Tony O'Reilly

5. **France lost 6–16 to Wales in February 2013. Who scored the only try of the match?**
    a) George North
    b) Justin Tipuric
    c) Richard Hibbard

6. **South Africa defeated Western Samoa 42–14 in 1995. Who scored four tries in the game?**
    a) Gavin Johnson
    b) Chester Williams
    c) Hendrik le Roux

7. **In 1989, who did Japan defeat 28–24 in Tokyo?**
    a) Australia
    b) Scotland
    c) Wales

8. **Which future Scarlets centre became the first player in rugby union's professional era to make his New Zealand debut before playing a game of Super Rugby?**

9. **Bath beat Leicester 16–15 in the 1996 Pilkington Cup final. Who received a six-month ban for pushing over referee Steve Lander at the end of the game?**

10. **Who was named International Rugby Board coach of the year for a record fifth occasion in 2011?**

Round 8

1. **Mark Loane, Mervyn Davies and Andy Ripley were all known for playing at which position?**
   a) Centre
   b) Number 8
   c) Hooker

2. **Who captained Australia 55 times in 86-capped appearances from 1991 until 2001?**
   a) Jason Little
   b) Tim Horan
   c) John Eales

3. **Who co-presented the 1997 and 1998 series of UK *Gladiators* with Ulrika Jonsson?**
   a) Jeremy Guscott
   b) Ieuan Evans
   c) Scott Hastings

4. **Cardigan Fields, Headingley and Meanwood Road are grounds that have hosted England internationals. In which city were these located?**
   a) Manchester
   b) Leeds
   c) Bristol

5. **Which Going brother scored 714 points in 130 matches for North Auckland from 1963 until 1975?**
   a) Sid
   b) Ken
   c) Brian

6. **Ireland dual international (rugby union and football) Kevin O'Flanagan played football for which of the following clubs?**

    a) Manchester United
    b) Liverpool
    c) Arsenal

7. **Peter Williams was an England rugby union international and Wales rugby league international. His father was a former Llanelli forward. Who was his father?**

    a) Ossie Williams
    b) Rhys (RH) Williams
    c) Roy Williams

8. **In 1992, who set a Scottish record of 25 appearances as national captain?**

9. **Who in 2011 became the first New Zealand international to achieve 100 caps?**

10. **John Philip Botha made his South Africa debut in November 2002 against France. What nickname is he better known by?**

Round 9

1. **Which country has a red rose as its badge on its shirt?**
   a) England
   b) Ireland
   c) Wales

2. **Vern Cotter became Scotland head coach in 2014. Who held the position on an interim basis prior to this?**
   a) Gareth Jenkins
   b) Scott Johnson
   c) Mike Ruddock

3. **Who did Italy beat 23–18 at Stadio Olimpico in the 2013 Six Nations championship?**
   a) Ireland
   b) Wales
   c) France

4. **Wales beat Scotland 23–26 at Murrayfield in 2015. Who scored the two Welsh tries?**
   a) Leigh Halfpenny and Alex Cuthbert
   b) Rhys Webb and Jonathan Davies
   c) Gethin Jenkins and Liam Williams

5. **Who captained South Africa for the only occasion in his 25th and final Test, a 9–18 loss to England at Ellis Park in 1972?**
   a) Piet Greyling
   b) Syd Nomis
   c) Jan Ellis

6. **France lost 13–18 to Argentina at Stade de France in November 2014. Who scored 15 points for the visitors?**

   a) Juan Martín Hernández
   b) Santiago Gonzáles Iglesias
   c) Nicolás Sánchez

7. **Who won the inaugural Women's Rugby World Cup in 1991?**

   a) USA
   b) France
   c) Netherlands

8. **Which South Africa winger was named International Rugby Board player of the year in 2007?**

9. **Who scored 645 points in 46 New Zealand Tests from 1985 until 1993?**

10. **Rhys Williams won European Championship 400m hurdles gold in 2012. Who is his father?**

Round 10

1. **Rugby football is a game for gentlemen in all classes, but for no bad sportsman in any class. This is the motto for which club?**
   - a) Hawick
   - b) Barbarians
   - c) Penarth

2. **Which of the following clubs did Rob Andrew not play for?**
   - a) Wasps
   - b) Nottingham
   - c) Richmond

3. **BBC commentator Bill McLaren was asked in 2002 to select his greatest ever world XV. Who did he select at full-back?**
   - a) Andy Irvine
   - b) JPR Williams
   - c) Serge Blanco

4. **Who played his last international match in 1983 having scored a record for a prop of eight tries in 55 games?**
   - a) Graham Price
   - b) Robert Paparemborde
   - c) Mike Burton

5. **Which club set a world record by scoring 1,917 points in a 50-game season in 1988/89?**

     a) Neath

     b) Bath

     c) Dolphin

6. **Who kicked a last-minute drop-goal to give Scotland a one-point victory over Italy in 2014?**

     a) Ruaridh Jackson

     b) Stuart Hogg

     c) Duncan Weir

7. **Which side did Ian McIntosh coach to their first Currie Cup final victory with an 18–12 defeat of Northern Transvaal?**

     a) Natal

     b) Western Province

     c) Free State

8. **Brian O'Brien had the distinction of becoming Shannon's first Ireland international in 1968. Which position did he play on his debut?**

9. **Who scored 19 tries in 34 Test matches for New Zealand from 1977 to 1983?**

10. **Who captained Fiji to victories at the 1997 and 2005 Rugby World Cup Sevens?**

Round 11

1. Who are the 'Sea Eagles'?

   a) Tonga

   b) Papua New Guinea

   c) France

2. In 2013, who became the first player to exceed 1,500 points in Super Rugby?

   a) Dan Carter

   b) Morné Steyn

   c) Tony Brown

3. Who replaced Jason Leonard during England's 54–21 victory over Italy in 1996, becoming his country's first tactical substitute?

   a) Graham Rowntree

   b) Rob Hardwick

   c) John Mallett

4. Who denied Wales a 1969 Five Nations Grand Slam with an 8–8 draw?

   a) Ireland

   b) Scotland

   c) France

5. Italy beat Samoa 24–13 in November 2014. Who kicked 14 Italian points on his Test debut?

   a) Tobie Botes

   b) Tommaso Allan

   c) Kelly Haimona

6. **Who made a world record 64th Test appearance in Wales' 20–16 victory over Ireland in 1978?**

   a) Gareth Edwards
   b) Mike Gibson
   c) Gerald Davies

7. **Which Nadi-born player ended his Fiji career in 2010 with 16 tries from 47 internationals?**

   a) Norman Ligairi
   b) Albert Vulivuli
   c) Gaby Lovobalavu

8. **Who set a world record 911 points tally from a 72-Test career for Australia from 1985 to 1995?**

9. **40 times capped Scotland international Hugh McLeod was known as a one-club man. Who did he both play for and was president of?**

10. **Ireland won the 2014 Six Nations championship. Who won the Triple Crown?**

Round 12

1. **Which colour shirt did France wear in the 2015 Six Nations for the first time since 1959?**
   a) Black
   b) White
   c) Red

2. **Lord Kew, Basil Brush and Le Hippy were nicknames given to which Welsh back-row forward?**
   a) John Taylor
   b) Dai Morris
   c) Paul Ringer

3. **South Africa beat Italy 101–0 in June 1999. Who in the match became the first Springbok to score five tries in an international?**
   a) Breyton Paulse
   b) Stefan Terblanche
   c) Robbie Fleck

4. **Who lost 25–9 to Georgia at the 2011 Rugby World Cup?**
   a) Scotland
   b) Romania
   c) Ireland

5. **Which member of New Zealand's 1987 Rugby World Cup winning team had a father, Brian, who won three Test caps in the 1950s?**
   a) Sean Fitzpatrick
   b) John Gallagher
   c) Warwick Taylor

6. **In which year did Scotland gain their first Triple Crown?**

    a) 1891
    b) 1911
    c) 1931

7. **Ireland fielded a three-quarter line of Jack Arigho, Eugene Davy, Morgan Crowe and Ned Lightfoot during their 1931 season. Which club did they all play for?**

    a) Cork Constitution
    b) Old Belvedere
    c) Lansdowne

8. **Which scrum-half made 36 Test appearances for Australia between 1968 and 1982?**

9. **At the age of 36, who became England's oldest centre when he played against his country of birth, South Africa, in 2007?**

10. **Name the Ebbw Vale back-row forward who made his Wales debut in 1977 against Ireland.**

Round 13

1. **Arorangi Cowboys and Titikaveka Bulls are clubs from which country?**
   - a) Cook Islands
   - b) Spain
   - c) Tonga

2. **Who did Japan defeat for the first time in their history 23–8 in June 2013?**
   - a) South Africa
   - b) Wales
   - c) France

3. **Who was captain of South Africa's 'Invincibles' tour of Australia in 1971 where they never lost a game?**
   - a) Piet Greyling
   - b) Frik du Preez
   - c) Hannes Marais

4. **Wales defeated France for a fourth consecutive time in 2015. In which year did they last achieve this?**
   - a) 1927
   - b) 1957
   - c) 1977

5. **Who played the last of his record 67 USA internationals, in a game against Italy in 2012?**
   - a) Mike MacDonald
   - b) Paul Emerick
   - c) Mike Hercus

6. **In 1997, which country lost 51–16 to Fiji at Suva?**

   a) Wales
   b) Italy
   c) Scotland

7. **Who set a New South Wales try scoring record of 49 touchdowns in 82 matches in a career that spanned from 1926 to 1938?**

   a) Allen Bowers
   b) Cyril Towers
   c) Jock Blackwood

8. **From 1967 until 1978, who set a Scotland record of playing in 49 consecutive internationals?**

9. **Munster defeated Australia 11–8 at Musgrave Park in 1967. Who captained the side?**

10. **Which former All Black became the host of the *Brunch* programme on New Zealand's Choice TV in 2012?**

Round 14

1. **In 2012, which country joined the Tri-Nations to form The Rugby Championship?**
    - a) Kenya
    - b) Argentina
    - c) Samoa

2. **France defeated Australia 30–24 in the 1987 Rugby World Cup semi-final. Who scored the winning try?**
    - a) Patrice Lagisquet
    - b) Pascal Ondarts
    - c) Serge Blanco

3. **In which country were New Zealand internationals Greg Rawlinson and Andrew Mehrtens born?**
    - a) India
    - b) South Africa
    - c) Saudi Arabia

4. **22-year-old George North, in 2015, became the youngest player to earn 50 international caps. Whose record did he supersede?**
    - a) Ma'a Nonu
    - b) Jonny Wilkinson
    - c) Joe Roff

5. **Who coached the Crusaders to five Super Rugby championships from 2000 to 2008?**
    - a) Robbie Deans
    - b) Wayne Smith
    - c) Peter Sloane

6. **During the 2002 European Cup final Leicester Tigers were defending their line with minutes to go. Munster had an attacking scrum. What happened next?**

   a) As Munster's Peter Stringer fed the ball into the scrum, Leicester's Neil Back knocked it out of his grasp without the referee seeing.

   b) The referee yellow carded Munster's John Hayes for bringing down the scrum. Leicester gained 40 metres from the resulting penalty.

   c) Referee whistled for full time three minutes early.

7. **In 1981, who became the first northern hemisphere side to win the Hong Kong Sevens and also the last non-international side to win the tournament?**

   a) Public School Wanderers

   b) Barbarians

   c) Co-optimists

8. **Lawrence Dallaglio won 85 caps in his England career. Which other two countries did he qualify for?**

9. **Wales selected a pair of uncapped outside-halves for their 1978 tour of Australia. Who were they?**

10. **Scotland flanker Rob Wainwright was a double Cambridge blue. One was for rugby union. What was the other for?**

Round 15

1. **Which country did Nick Popplewell, Jim Staples and Niall Hogan represent?**

   a) Samoa

   b) USA

   c) Ireland

2. **Stuart Lancaster was named permanent England head coach in 2012. Which country did he represent in his playing career at under-19 and under-20 level?**

   a) Scotland

   b) Wales

   c) Kenya

3. **Who was South Africa's first captain following their re-admission to international rugby in 1992?**

   a) Heinrich Rodgers

   b) Uli Schmidt

   c) Naas Botha

4. **Which country defeated France 12–17 in the group stages of the 2007 Rugby World Cup?**

   a) Argentina

   b) Wales

   c) Fiji

5. **Marc Cécillon, the former France back-row forward was sent to jail in 2004 and served seven years of his sentence. What was he convicted of doing?**

a) Running a human trafficking enterprise.

b) Murdering his wife.

c) Being caught on a boat transporting $50 million of cocaine into Portugal.

6. Who captained Australia to their first Bledisloe Cup victory on New Zealand soil in 1949?

a) Rex Mossop

b) Jack Blomley

c) Trevor Allan

7. What was unusual about Llanelli's Emrys Evans' three-cap Wales career from 1937 to 1939?

a) He played at prop in the first international and as a flanker in the others.

b) On all three occasions he was called into the team as an on-the-day replacement for an injured colleague.

c) He played with a different brother on each occasion.

8. Pedro Carvalho became his country's first ever try scorer in a Rugby World Cup during a 56–10 loss to Scotland in 2007. Which country did he play for?

9. Who made his New Zealand debut in 1974 at the age of 29, captaining his country in all 10 Tests that he played?

10. Jason Leonard achieved a milestone in 2003 that only three others had ever achieved in an England shirt. The other three were Dave Davies and Cyril Lowe in 1923, and Ron Cove-Smith in 1928. What was this achievement?

Round 16

1. **Which country is known as 'The Cherry Blossoms'?**

    a) Japan

    b) Samoa

    c) Namibia

2. **The last day of the 2015 Six Nations tournament saw a new record set for the most tries scored in a single day of the competition. How many tries were scored on 21 March 2015?**

    a) 21

    b) 25

    c) 27

3. **Who set a national record of captaining France on 34 occasions between 1977 and 1984?**

    a) Gérard Cholley

    b) Jean-Pierre Rives

    c) Jean-Claude Skrela

4. **England defeated the Netherlands 110–0 in November 1998. Who set a national record of 15 conversions on the day?**

    a) Paul Grayson

    b) Jonny Wilkinson

    c) Tim Stimpson

5. Which Welsh front-row forward scored nine tries in 41 British and Irish Lions matches from 1955 to 1962?

    a) Billy Williams
    b) Bryn Meredith
    c) Courtney Meredith

6. Which side became the first opponents of the Barbarians on the 27th of December 1890?

    a) Cardiff
    b) Devon County
    c) Hartlepool Rovers

7. Which scrum-half played in 12 Tests for Australia from 1958 to 1959, then went on to earn the same number of caps for New Zealand from 1961 to 1964?

    a) Ken McMullen
    b) Brian Cox
    c) Des Connor

8. Who missed a straightforward penalty kick in front of the posts for Scotland as they lost 6–9 to England in the 1991 Rugby World Cup semi-final?

9. 'Viet Gwent' was the nickname given to which Welsh club's front-row during the 1970s?

10. Who scored 20 points on his New Zealand debut against Wales at Hamilton in 2003?

Round 17

1. **Girvan Dempsey scored 19 tries in 82 international appearances. Which country did he represent?**
    - a) Samoa
    - b) Ireland
    - c) Scotland

2. **Who scored an Argentina record of 651 points in 87 matches from 1998 to 2013?**
    - a) Felipe Contepomi
    - b) Juan Fernández Miranda
    - c) Federico Todeschini

3. **Newlands is a stadium that hosted its first South Africa international match in 1891. In which city is it located?**
    - a) Polokwane
    - b) Nelspruit
    - c) Cape Town

4. **Which member of New Zealand's 2007 Rugby World Cup squad had a father Frank who earned 17 Test caps for the All Blacks from 1976 to 1981?**
    - a) Leon MacDonald
    - b) Byron Kelleher
    - c) Anton Oliver

5. **Prop Ron Jacobs made a record 470 club appearances from 1949 to 1966. Which club did he represent during this period?**

      a) Northampton

      b) Moseley

      c) Coventry

6. **Oscar winning actor Javier Bardem won under-16 and under-18 caps for which country?**

      a) Spain

      b) Argentina

      c) Uruguay

7. **Who scored eight tries in 12 matches on the 1974 British and Irish Lions tour of South Africa?**

      a) Gordon Brown

      b) Willie John McBride

      c) Chris Ralston

8. **Gavin Henson left Ospreys in 2010 to join which English club side?**

9. **Who played his last international match in 1997, finishing his career as New Zealand's highest try-scoring Test forward with 17 touchdowns in 58 appearances?**

10. **Arturo Bergamasco won four caps for Italy in the 1970s. Who are his two international sons?**

Round 18

1. **Wycliff Palu, Scott Quinnell and Anthony Foley have all made over 50 appearances for their country. Which position would you associate with them?**

    a) Hooker

    b) Scrum-half

    c) Number 8

2. **Which former international held the role of Argentina's Minister of Sport from 1996 until 1999?**

    a) Gustavo Milano

    b) Hugo Porta

    c) Raul Loyola

3. **What did the following hookers have in common: Bath's Andy Long, Newbridge's Ken Waters and Hawick's Jim Hay?**

    a) They were once-capped internationals.

    b) They won a British and Irish Lions cap before playing for their country.

    c) They won international caps at two different positions but not as a hooker.

4. **Which Australian was named the inaugural International Rugby Board coach of the year in 2001?**

    a) Greg Smith

    b) Eddie Jones

    c) Rod Macqueen

5. Who made the last of 63 appearances for Samoa in a 12–73 victory over Papua New Guinea in 2009?

   a) Semo Sititi
   b) Lolo Lui
   c) Uale Mai

6. Who scored a try with his first touch in international rugby after just a minute of his debut in New Zealand's 59–10 win over Italy in November 2004?

   a) Joe Rokocoko
   b) Conrad Smith
   c) Ma'a Nonu

7. Captain Walter Rees became secretary of the Welsh Rugby Union in 1896. How long did he stay in this position?

   a) 32 years
   b) 42 years
   c) 52 years

8. Who retired in 1973 as Ireland's most capped player (55 games) and having made the most appearances as captain (22 games)?

9. Who scored 12 tries in 33 Scotland matches from 1955 until 1962?

10. Gysie Piennar earned 13 caps for South Africa in the early 1980s. His son made his international debut in August 2006. Who is the younger Piennar?

Round 19

1. **Who scored 1,083 points in 128 Ireland appearances?**
    - a) David Humphreys
    - b) Paddy Wallace
    - c) Ronan O'Gara

2. **Flanker Jamie Joseph played international rugby for which two countries?**
    - a) Scotland and Samoa
    - b) New Zealand and Japan
    - c) Wales and Papua New Guinea

3. **Wales romped to a 51–3 victory over Scotland in 2014. Which member of the opposition was sent off 23 minutes into the game for a late shoulder charge on Dan Biggar?**
    - a) Stuart Hogg
    - b) Dougie Fife
    - c) Alex Dunbar

4. **South Africa prop Ollie le Roux left the Cheetahs in 2007 to ply his trade in Europe. Which team did he join?**
    - a) Cardiff Blues
    - b) Worcester Warriors
    - c) Leinster

5. **Who retired at the age of 38 in 1967 as Australia's most capped player with 41 appearances?**
    - a) Jim Lenehan
    - b) Tony Miller
    - c) Eddie Stapleton

6. **Full-back Ken Scotland made 27 international appearances for the Scotland rugby union team. Which other sport did he play internationally?**

      a) Cricket

      b) Rugby league

      c) Basketball

7. **Coventry wing Timothy Dalton won his only England cap in 1969 during an 8–3 victory over Scotland. He became the first Englishman to earn a cap as a substitute. Who did he replace in the game?**

      a) Keith Fielding

      b) Rodney Webb

      c) Bob Hiller

8. **The British and Irish Lions drew the first Test of their 1971 tour against New Zealand 14–14. Which Welshman kicked a fantastic 45-metre drop-goal, the only one of his illustrious career during the game?**

9. **The Madejski Stadium in Reading became home to which club side in 2000?**

10. **Who presented the Webb Ellis Cup to Francois Piennar at the end of the 1995 Rugby World Cup final?**

Round 20

1. **Who made his 100th and final appearance for Wales against the Barbarians in 2012?**

   a) Martyn Williams

   b) Lee Byrne

   c) Dwayne Peel

2. **Joe Schmidt became head coach of which country in 2013?**

   a) Samoa

   b) Ireland

   c) Namibia

3. **Who lost 38–23 to England in the 1994 Women's Rugby World Cup final?**

   a) Canada

   b) Wales

   c) USA

4. **Which Australia back-row forward played in 59 Tests including four as captain from 1980 until 1991?**

   a) David Codey

   b) Simon Poidevin

   c) Troy Coker

5. **Mark Keyworth, Tony Swift and Maurice Colclough won England caps while playing for which Welsh side?**

   a) Aberavon

   b) Ebbw Vale

   c) Swansea

6. **Who were the inaugural winners of the Hong Kong Sevens Cup in 1976?**

    a) Fiji

    b) Cantabrians

    c) Indonesia

7. **Which South Africa centre scored ten tries in 38 international matches from 1996 to 2006?**

    a) Japie Mulder

    b) Marius Joubert

    c) Andre Snyman

8. **Which winger of Polynesian decent scored 71 points in 38 All Black Tests from 1970 until 1978?**

9. **Which French side did Cardiff Blues defeat 28–21 to win the 2010 European Challenge Cup?**

10. **Who set a Canada record of 491 points in a 55-match international career that spanned from 1986 until 1999?**

Round 21

1. **What's the colour of Tonga's home shirt?**
   a) Red
   b) Blue
   c) White

2. **The Highlanders play home matches in which of the following cities?**
   a) Auckland
   b) Dunedin
   c) Napier

3. **Which club side won the French championship six times during the 1970s?**
   a) Beziers
   b) Narbonne
   c) Dax

4. **What was interesting about Daniel Carroll's two rugby Olympic gold medals?**
   a) He won the first for Australasia in 1908 and the second for the USA in 1920.
   b) On both occasions he wasn't in the original squad but drafted in as an emergency replacement.
   c) There was a record 24-year gap between his first and second victories.

5. **What on-field controversy occurred during England's 35–22 victory over Samoa in the 2003 Rugby World Cup?**

a) Hooker Mark Regan played for England. Due to a red card in the previous match he was suspended but the England management didn't realise and selected him for the match.

b) England played 30 seconds with 16 players on the field.

c) Flanker Neil Back illegally used his hands in an attacking scrum resulting in England incorrectly being awarded a penalty try.

6. **Sean Fitzpatrick suffered an ear bite when playing against South Africa in 1994. The aggressor received an 18-month ban. Who received the ban?**

   a) Tiaan Strauss
   b) Krynauw Otto
   c) Johan le Roux

7. **Mike Catt, Austin Healey and Josh Lewsey have all made over 50 appearances for England. What feat have each accomplished while playing for their country?**

   a) Started a match in four different positions.
   b) Kicked a hat-trick of drop-goals in a match.
   c) Gained more caps coming off the bench than starting a game.

8. **Who played in his 141st and final international match during Ireland's 2014 victory over France?**

9. **Which member of Wales' 1965 Triple Crown winning side signed for the Buffalo Bills American football side as a specialist kicker in 1971?**

10. **Jim Thompson scored a try on his Scotland A debut in 2008. Who was his Scottish rugby hall of fame grandfather?**

Round 22

1. **Who played the last of his 59 Irish appearances in a 78–9 win over Japan in November 2000?**

   a) Dominic Crotty
   b) Paddy Johns
   c) Ross Nesdale

2. **Which country defeated New Zealand 43–31 in a 1999 Rugby World Cup semi-final?**

   a) France
   b) Wales
   c) South Africa

3. **The Cavaliers were an unofficial New Zealand team that toured South Africa in 1986. Who was the team coach?**

   a) Colin Meads
   b) Ian Kirkpatrick
   c) Sid Going

4. **France overcame England 26–24 in February 2014. Which teenage centre came off the bench to score the winning try with three minutes left on the clock?**

   a) François Fontaine
   b) Léo Ghirard
   c) Gaël Fickou

5. **England defeated Wales 11–6 at Twickenham in 1910. Who set a national record for fastest scoring debut try scorer by crossing the whitewash 75 seconds into the match?**
   - a) Bert Solomon
   - b) Fred Chapman
   - c) Edgar Mobbs

6. **Who scored Australia's only try in their 1991 Rugby World Cup final victory over England?**
   - a) Marty Roebuck
   - b) Tony Daly
   - c) Willie Ofahengaue

7. **BBC Wales awarded their first 'Wales Sports Personality Of The Year' award in 1954. Who won it?**
   - a) Roy John
   - b) Cliff Morgan
   - c) Ken Jones

8. **The English County Championship competition was renamed in 2007 to honour a former international. Who was it named after?**

9. **Future Wallaby head coach Michael Cheika guided which Irish province to their first European Cup final in 2009?**

10. **New Zealand defeated Samoa 71–13 in June 1999. Which pair of brothers found themselves on opposing sides that day?**

Round 23

1. **In which country would you find Free State Stadium and Kingspark?**

   a) Wales

   b) South Africa

   c) Italy

2. **Simon Raiwalui, Emori Katalau and Kele Leawere are all Fiji internationals. Which position would you associate with them?**

   a) Scrum-half

   b) Full-back

   c) Second-row

3. **Who led Ireland to their first Grand Slam in 1948?**

   a) Karl Mullen

   b) Barney Mullan

   c) Jack Kyle

4. **Mike Campbell-Lamerton relinquished the British and Irish Lions captaincy for two Tests on their 1966 tour because he felt he wasn't playing well enough. Who was given the captaincy for those matches?**

   a) Dewi Bebb

   b) Delme Thomas

   c) David Watkins

5. **England internationals William Milton, Reggie Schwartz and Reginald Hands share what in common?**

   a) They won their first cap while still at school.
   b) They were also South Africa cricket internationals.
   c) They earned caps for England while representing five different clubs.

6. **Which Australian gained nine caps in a 13-week international career, which culminated with winning the 1991 Rugby World Cup final?**

   a) Bob Egerton
   b) Paul Carozza
   c) Darren Junee

7. **Merab Kvirikashvili scored a national record 32 points against Germany in 2010. Which country was he playing for?**

   a) Georgia
   b) Romania
   c) Czech Republic

8. **Brothers Dolf, Jaap and Martiens Bekker were all international rugby players. Which country did they represent?**

9. **Sam Warburton captained Wales for a record 34th time in 2015. Whose record did he overtake?**

10. **Wales beat England 21–19 in January 1981. Who scored all 19 points for the visitors?**

Round 24

1. **In 1970, who became the first All Black to play in 50 Tests?**
    - a) Ian Clarke
    - b) Colin Meads
    - c) Kelvin Tremain

2. **Craig Chalmers, Keith Robertson and Jim Telfer all played for which club side?**
    - a) Stirling County
    - b) Melrose
    - c) Boroughmuir

3. **Gloucester played Exeter University on 15 November 1978 at Kingsholm. Who made the first of 301 appearances for the 'Cherry and Whites' that day?**
    - a) John Gadd
    - b) John Orwin
    - c) Mike Teague

4. **Which of the following Welshmen made the most Test appearances for the British and Irish Lions?**
    - a) John Taylor
    - b) Jeff Squire
    - c) Derek Quinnell

5. **Which future Wallaby became Australia's youngest ever rugby league international when he played for the Kangaroos against New Zealand in 2007?**

   a) Israel Folau
   b) Joe Tomane
   c) Henry Speight

6. **Which club won the French championship in 2009 for the first time in 54 years?**

   a) Grenoble
   b) Colomiers
   c) Perpignan

7. **Wales defeated France 13–20 at Stade de France in 2015. Who scored his first international try on his 31st appearance in a Welsh shirt in the match?**

   a) Dan Biggar
   b) Luke Charteris
   c) Taulupe Faletau

8. **Thomond Park is home to both Shannon and UL Bohemian. In which city is the stadium located?**

9. **Who retired from Test rugby in 2008 as South Africa's highest point scorer (893 points)?**

10. **Jeff Wilson scored 234 points in 60 New Zealand Test matches. In which other sport did he represent his country?**

Round 25

1. **Ireland won back-to-back Six Nations championships in 2015. When was the last time an Irish side achieved this (during the Five Nations era)?**

    a) 1929

    b) 1949

    c) 1969

2. **Which Wales forward earned 46 caps in an international career that spanned from 1985 until 1995?**

    a) Mike Griffiths

    b) David Bryant

    c) Phil Davies

3. **Which of the following South Africa scrum-halves earned the highest number of caps?**

    a) Piet Uys

    b) Dawie de Villiers

    c) Dick Lockyear

4. **On the 18 April 1892 Stade Français hosted the first game on continental Europe for an English side. Which of the following was the pioneering side that won the game by four converted tries to nil?**

    a) Rosslyn Park

    b) Oxford University

    c) Blackheath

5. **Whose Wallaby debut lasted only 42 seconds as his head made contact with Jonathan Davies' hip in the 2013 first Test against the British and Irish Lions?**

    a) Tevita Kuridrani
    b) Israel Folau
    c) Christian Lealiifano

6. **In which country was the Escott Shield first competed for in 1913 and won by the Pacific club?**

    a) Fiji
    b) Japan
    c) Tonga

7. **Which international hooker was jailed for six months in 1995 for fracturing an opponent's jaw?**

    a) Louis Armary
    b) Nigel Meek
    c) Tom Lawton

8. **Who coached France to the 2011 Rugby World Cup final?**

9. **In 2011, who became the second Argentine to be inducted into the International Rugby Board hall of fame?**

10. **Ray Dalton and his son Andy were both New Zealand internationals. Which of them won the most caps?**

Round 26

1. **Which country performs the Haka war dance before international matches?**
    a) Australia
    b) New Zealand
    c) Japan

2. **Who overtook Stephen Jones as Wales' most capped international with his 105th appearance in 2014?**
    a) James Hook
    b) Adam Jones
    c) Gethin Jenkins

3. **In 1999, who became the first Scotland player to score a try in all four Five Nations games in a season?**
    a) Gregor Townsend
    b) John Leslie
    c) Kenny Logan

4. **How many caps in total were won by Malcolm O'Kelly (1997–2009), Mark Taylor (1994–2005) and Olivier Roumat (1989–1996)?**
    a) 205
    b) 238
    c) 263

5. **Who scored both tries as South Africa defeated New Zealand 14–3 in August 1970?**

   a) Piet Visagie

   b) Ian McCallum

   c) Gert Muller

6. **Who was the only member of England's squad to play every minute of their 2003 Rugby World Cup winning campaign?**

   a) Ben Kay

   b) Lawrence Dallaglio

   c) Trevor Woodman

7. **Once-capped Welsh internationals Gordon Britton, Laurie Daniel and Roy Burnett all played for which club side?**

   a) Ebbw Vale

   b) Pontypool

   c) Newport

8. **Avril Williams made his international debut in June 1984. For which country did he become the second black player to represent them?**

9. **Following Gareth Edwards' famous try for the Barbarians against the All Blacks in 1973, who in the BBC commentary said 'If the greatest writer of the written word would have written that story, no one would have believed it'?**

10. **France defeated Zimbabwe 70–12 in June 1987. Who scored a French record 30 points in the match?**

Round 27

1. **Ellis Park is a stadium located in which city?**

   a) Johannesburg

   b) Port Elizabeth

   c) Kimberley

2. **Luke McLean made his international debut in June 2008. Which country did he represent when taking to the field that day?**

   a) Italy

   b) Samoa

   c) Tonga

3. **Who earned 92 Welsh caps in an international career that spanned from 1989 until 2004?**

   a) Scott Gibbs

   b) John Davies

   c) Gareth Llewellyn

4. **Which of the following countries did not appear at the 2010 Women's Rugby World Cup?**

   a) Sweden

   b) Fiji

   c) Kazakhstan

5. **Former Pontypridd coach Lynn Howells became director of rugby for which national team in 2012?**

   a) Romania

   b) Portugal

   c) Japan

6. **Alexander Obolensky became the first Englishman to score a brace of tries against the All Blacks on his debut in 1936. Robert Lloyd became the second Englishman to do this in 1967. Who became the third in 2008?**

   a) Dan Hipkiss
   b) Topsy Ojo
   c) Ugo Monye

7. **In 1857, which was the first club to be founded in Scotland?**

   a) Glasgow Academicals
   b) West of Scotland
   c) Edinburgh Academicals

8. **Who defeated Clarence Tillman in 2012 to become New Zealand's heavyweight boxing champion?**

9. **Andrew David James made 42 South Africa appearances from 2001 until 2011. By which nickname is he better known?**

10. **Who set a French record of 265 points during a 34-Test career in the 1970s?**

Round 28

1. **Which country won the first four Commonwealth Games Sevens tournaments from 1998 to 2010?**

    a) Fiji

    b) New Zealand

    c) Scotland

2. **South Africa prop Tendai Mtawarira made his debut against Wales in 2008. By which nickname is he better known?**

    a) T-bone

    b) Gonzo

    c) Beast

3. **David Denton, Bobby Skinstad and Takudzwa Ngwenya were all born in which country?**

    a) Zimbabwe

    b) Burkina Faso

    c) Kenya

4. **Hoylake Rugby Club boasts which James Bond actor as a former player?**

    a) Roger Moore

    b) Timothy Dalton

    c) Daniel Craig

5. **England beat Romania 22–15 at Twickenham in January 1985. Who on his debut set a record for the fastest England drop-goal, 47 seconds into the game?**

    a) Rob Andrew
    b) Stuart Barnes
    c) Nick Stringer

6. **Which 30 times capped Australian forward was awarded the Order of the British Empire in 1971, became Lord Mayor of Sydney in 1973, was knighted in 1976 and made a Companion of the Order of Australia in 1990?**

    a) Jim Walsh
    b) Nicholas Shehadie
    c) Peter Fenwicke

7. **Which 53 times capped USA international played for sides including Overmarch Parma, Newport Gwent Dragons, Ulster and Wasps?**

    a) David Fee
    b) Kort Schubert
    c) Paul Emerick

8. **Stade Marcel-Michelin is the home ground for which club side?**

9. **England defeated Italy 47–17 in February 2015. Who became England's oldest ever try scorer in the match?**

10. **Which country required a last-minute penalty to scrape a 3–3 draw against Munster at Musgrave Park in 1973?**

Round 29

1. **England internationals Henry Paul, Lesley Vainikolo and Shontayne Hape were all rugby league internationals prior to their move to union. Which country did they represent in the 13-man code?**

   a) Samoa

   b) New Zealand

   c) Scotland

2. **The book *Talk of the Toony* was released in 2007. Whose autobiography was it?**

   a) Kenny Logan

   b) Jim Telfer

   c) Gregor Townsend

3. **Which of the following finished his New Zealand career with a national record of 49 tries achieved in 61 Test appearances?**

   a) Doug Howlett

   b) Christian Cullen

   c) Joe Rokocoko

4. **What do South Africa internationals Basie Vivier, Wynand Claassen and Corné Krige have in common?**

   a) Born in Scotland.

   b) Captained the Springboks on their debut.

   c) The only players to have represented South Africa while playing for four different sides.

5. **Wales crushed Italy 20–61 at Rome in the 2015 Six Nations tournament. Who scored a ten-minute hat-trick of tries in the second half?**

    a) Scott Williams

    b) Jamie Roberts

    c) George North

6. **Roland Bertranne set a French record in the 1970s by playing in the most consecutive Tests. How many matches did he play during this run?**

    a) 36

    b) 41

    c) 46

7. **Who in 1980 became the first Shannon player to represent the British and Irish Lions?**

    a) Colm Tucker

    b) Brendan Foley

    c) Gerry McLoughlin

8. **How many Scotland defenders did Ieuan Evans overcome to score a famous try in Wales' 25–20 win in 1988?**

9. **Who defeated France to gain third place at the 2007 Rugby World Cup?**

10. *Wild Women Of Wongo* **was a 1958 Hollywood film. Which former Wales international played the role of the King of Wongo?**

Round 30

1. **Denis Dallan, Alessandro Troncon and Cristian Stoica have all played international rugby for which country?**
    a) Ireland
    b) Italy
    c) Georgia

2. **Ireland lost 15–16 to Wales at Lansdowne Road in 1992. Who were the opposing captains?**
    a) Phillip Matthews and Ieuan Evans
    b) Donal Lenihan and Mike Hall
    c) Brendan Mullin and Garin Jenkins

3. **What did Australian referee Bob Burnett say to Welsh scrum-half Brynmor Williams during Australia's 18–8 victory over Wales in 1978?**
    a) 'It's not your ball Williams, it's ours.'
    b) 'Don't bother trying. This will be a gold victory.'
    c) 'I'm not here to let you win.'

4. **Naas Botha played 28 Test matches for South Africa as a fly-half. What has he had named after him?**
    a) A planet
    b) A rose
    c) A highway

5. **Who was the only player never to have been dropped during Clive Woodward's reign as England head coach?**
    a) Jason Leonard
    b) Dan Luger
    c) Richard Hill

6. Who won a 100th New Zealand cap in 2013?

    a) Tony Woodcock

    b) Conrad Smith

    c) Kieran Read

7. Bath were English league champions for the 1991/92 season even though they had a point deducted. Why did they lose a point?

    a) They played 12 minutes of their home game against Nottingham with 16 players.

    b) They used an ineligible player, Laurie Heatherley, against London Irish.

    c) Their home ground, The Rec, failed a health and safety inspection resulting in the last-minute cancellation of their televised match with Orrell.

8. The Barbarians played their first international touring team at Cardiff Arms Park in January 1948. They won 9–6. Who was the opposition?

9. Who scored 44 points in Scotland's 89–0 victory over the Ivory Coast at the 1995 Rugby World Cup?

10. Eamonn Andrews presented the famous *This is your Life* red book to which player following Wales' 12–3 victory over England in 1972?

Round 31

1. **Which colour is the Samoa home rugby shirt?**
    a) Red and white hoops
    b) Blue
    c) Black

2. **In 2014, who became the first Welshman to sign a dual contract with the Welsh Rugby Union?**
    a) Tyler Morgan
    b) Dan Lydiate
    c) Sam Warburton

3. **Prior to 1924, what was the Scottish Rugby Union called?**
    a) Scottish Football Union
    b) Association of Scottish Rugby and Cricket clubs
    c) Scottish Rugby Committee

4. **Which country received a record five yellow cards during their 37–31 loss to Italy at Cremona in 2013?**
    a) Romania
    b) Tonga
    c) Fiji

5. **From 1875 to 1879 which country went a record ten matches without conceding a try?**
    a) England
    b) Scotland
    c) Wales

6. **For which Super Rugby side did Tana Umaga score 47 tries in 122 appearances from 1996 until 2007?**

   a) Crusaders
   b) Highlanders
   c) Hurricanes

7. **Thierry Lacroix set a France record of eight successful penalty kicks in a match in 1995. Who were the opposition?**

   a) South Africa
   b) Ireland
   c) Scotland

8. **Following Ireland's 18–9 victory over England in 1973, which member of the England team said 'Well we might not be any good, but at least we turned up'?**

9. **During the 1960s and 1970s which Wales flanker scored a club record 933 points for London Welsh?**

10. **Which city hosted the 2013 Rugby World Cup Sevens?**

Round 32

1. **John Kirwan, Kevin Skinner and Has Catley all played international rugby for which country?**

    a) New Zealand

    b) France

    c) Argentina

2. **How many caps did Chester Williams earn in a seven-year career for South Africa?**

    a) 27

    b) 34

    c) 41

3. **Fijian centre Seru Rabeni played for which English club side from 2004 until 2009?**

    a) Leeds Carnegie

    b) Leicester Tigers

    c) Gloucester

4. **Dick Thornett won international caps for Australia in both rugby union and league. He also represented his country at the 1960 Rome Olympics. What sport did he compete in?**

    a) Sailing

    b) Fencing

    c) Water polo

5. **In 2007, who was banned for life, later reduced to five years for assaulting an Ulster fan during a European Cup match between Toulouse and the men from Northern Ireland?**

   a) Yannick Bru
   b) Clément Poitrenaud
   c) Trevor Brennan

6. **Phil Bennett wrote a book in 2014 naming his greatest ever Scarlets XV. Who did he select at outside-half?**

   a) Himself
   b) Barry John
   c) Stephen Jones

7. **Which of the following scored the most international tries?**

   a) Émile Ntamack
   b) Christophe Dominici
   c) Christian Darrouy

8. **Who set a national record of 83 appearances as South Africa captain during a career that spanned 11 years from his Test debut against Canada in June 2000?**

9. **England's 1990 win over Argentina is remembered for Federico Mendez's thunderous right-hook which knocked out an England forward. Who was his victim?**

10. **The British and Irish Lions won their 1997 tour of South Africa by two Tests to one. Which Irish forward was voted players' player of the tour?**

Round 33

1. **For which country did Doddie Weir, James McLaren and Andy Reed all play international rugby?**

   a) Australia

   b) Scotland

   c) Ireland

2. **Which country performs the Sipi Tau war dance before games?**

   a) Tonga

   b) Japan

   c) Cook Islands

3. **Italian outside-half Kris Burton moved to Wales in 2013. Which side did he join?**

   a) Ospreys

   b) Pontypridd

   c) Newport Gwent Dragons

4. **Who did former Springbok coach Andre Markgraaff call the 'Eric Cantona of South Africa rugby' due to his controversial actions?**

   a) Pieter Muller

   b) Adriaan Richter

   c) James Small

5. How many international conversions were kicked in total by Luigi Troiani (1985–1995), Didier Camberabero (1982–1993) and Arwel Thomas (1996–2000)?

    a) 119

    b) 135

    c) 158

6. The Super Rugby championship was won by a South African side for the first time in 2007. Who were the champions?

    a) Bulls

    b) Stormers

    c) Sharks

7. In 1934, who became the first Australia captain to lift the Bledisloe Cup?

    a) Bill White

    b) Alec Ross

    c) Ron Walden

8. One-club man Mike Burton made 360 appearances for which side?

9. The 1981 film *Chariots of Fire* depicts the story of which Scottish international's gold medal win at the 1924 Olympic games?

10. What do JJ Williams' initials stand for?

Round 34

1. **Italian internationals Sergio Parisse, Mauro Bergamasco and Diego Domínguez have all played for which side?**
   a) Stade Français
   b) Melbourne Rebels
   c) Wasps

2. **Who scored a South Africa record of 35 points in a match against Namibia in 2007?**
   a) Morné Steyn
   b) Percy Montgomery
   c) Tonderai Chavhanga

3. **Jonah Lomu scored 37 tries in a 63-cap New Zealand career. Which country did he score the most against?**
   a) Australia
   b) Italy
   c) England

4. **Barry Holmes won six international caps, four for one country, two for another, got married and died, all in 1949. Which countries did he represent?**
   a) New Zealand and Scotland
   b) England and Argentina
   c) Wales and Australia

5. **Which Scotland international was elected to the South Africa parliament in 1974 as a member of the Progressive Party?**

   a) Stewart Wilson
   b) David Chisholm
   c) Gordon Waddell

6. **The Hopetoun Cup is contested by Australia and which other country?**

   a) Scotland
   b) Wales
   c) France

7. **Phil Orr finished his Ireland career as the world's most capped prop with 58 international appearances. Which club did he represent for over two decades?**

   a) Bective Rangers
   b) Old Wesley
   c) Lansdowne

8. **Which South Africa scrum-half played in the 1995, 1999 and 2003 Rugby World Cups?**

9. **Who became the oldest player to captain England for the first time at the age of 35 years and 175 days in August 2003?**

10. **Why was Andy Powell thrown out of Wales' 2010 Six Nations squad?**

Round 35

1. **Brothers Eddie and Ian Dunn, Robbie and Bruce Deans plus Rico and Hosea Gear have all gained international recognition. Which country have they represented?**

    a) Australia

    b) Tonga

    c) New Zealand

2. **Danie Craven, Kitch Christie and Peter de Villiers have all held the position of head coach for which country?**

    a) Italy

    b) South Africa

    c) Wales

3. **Where does Perpignan play home matches?**

    a) Stade Felix Mayol

    b) Stade Aimé Giral

    c) Stade Jean-Bouin

4. **José Maria Nuñez Piossek played his last international match in 2008 as his country's highest try scorer with 29 touchdowns in 28 games. Which country did he play for?**

    a) Argentina

    b) France

    c) Georgia

5. **During the British and Irish Lions tour of New Zealand in 1971, who scored a record six tries in a match for the tourists at Greymouth?**

    a) Mike Gibson
    b) David Duckham
    c) Gerald Davies

6. **Which founding club of the Rugby Football Union changed sports to football and won the FA Cup in 1880?**

    a) Queen's House
    b) Ravenscourt Park
    c) Clapham Rovers

7. **Singapore lost by a record score of 164–13 in October 1994. Who was the opposition?**

    a) New Zealand
    b) Hong Kong
    c) Japan

8. **Who scored 25 points for Australia in their 35–12 victory over France in the 1999 Rugby World Cup final?**

9. **Which club was the first to provide 100 players to the England international team?**

10. **Which Welsh international appeared as a contestant in the 2010 BBC series *Strictly Come Dancing*?**

Round 36

1. **Who captained Ireland a record 83 times from 2002 until 2012?**
    a) Rory Best
    b) Brian O'Driscoll
    c) Simon Easterby

2. **For which club side have Olivier Magne, Mike Blair and Alix Popham all represented?**
    a) Brive
    b) Edinburgh
    c) Benetton Treviso

3. **Which of the following scored the most points during their international career?**
    a) Thomas Castaignède
    b) Gérald Merceron
    c) Jean-Baptiste Élissalde

4. **Which of the following won the most Scotland caps?**
    a) Scott Hastings
    b) Jim Renwick
    c) Tom Smith

5. **At the age of 34, who became England's oldest scrum-half when he appeared against Fiji in 1988?**
    a) Michael Lampkowski
    b) Nigel Melville
    c) Richard Harding

6. **Tina Turner's 1985 hit 'We don't need another hero' contained backing vocals by a choir from King's House school. Which future England international was a member of the choir?**

   a) Joe Worsley
   b) Martin Johnson
   c) Lawrence Dallaglio

7. **England defeated South Africa 15–32 in June 1994. Who became the youngest ever Springbok prop at the age of 21 when he made his debut in the match?**

   a) Os du Randt
   b) Ollie le Roux
   c) Marius Hurter

8. **Reuben Thorne, Greg Somerville and Wyatt Crockett have each played over 100 matches for the same side. Which team was it?**

9. **Who became the second player to earn 100 Wales caps in a 28–31 loss to the Barbarians in 2011?**

10. **Who made a record 28 consecutive Test appearances for England from 1953 to 1959, helping his country to a first Grand Slam for 29 years in 1957?**

Round 37

1. **Which colour shirt do you associate with South Africa?**

   a) Red and silver
   b) Green and gold
   c) Blue and bronze

2. **Which Dunfermline-born Number 8 played the last of 20 internationals for Scotland in 1959?**

   a) Oliver Grant
   b) Jock Davidson
   c) Jim Greenwood

3. **Which country set a world record for the most capped pack when their side against Wales in 2014 contained forwards with a total of 587 appearances to their name?**

   a) Ireland
   b) Italy
   c) France

4. **Which New Zealand fly-half kicked all 18 points as Toulouse defeated Toulon by six points to win the 2012 French Top 14 championship?**

   a) Aaron Cruden
   b) Dan Carter
   c) Luke McAlister

5. **In which year did England first earn a Five Nations wooden spoon for losing all tournament games in a season?**

      a) 1967

      b) 1970

      c) 1972

6. **Who did England defeat 21–9 in the final of the 2014 Women's Rugby World Cup?**

      a) Australia

      b) Canada

      c) France

7. **In 1939, which country became the first to complete an unbeaten tour of New Zealand winning seven games and drawing one?**

      a) South Africa

      b) Fiji

      c) Australia

8. **Following a career that included 62 appearances for France, which 'caveman' announced his retirement in 2014?**

9. **Who played 25 Tests for Australia from 1980 to 1984, ten of which as captain, making him the first indigenous Australian to lead a national sporting team?**

10. **Who was the Newport lock that kicked a penalty goal in his only international to give Wales a 3–3 draw against Ireland in 1951?**

Round 38

1. **Marco Bollesan made 47 international appearances from 1963 until 1975 including 37 as captain. Which country did he represent?**

    a) Scotland

    b) Italy

    c) Australia

2. **Adrian Garvey made 28 appearances for South Africa from 1996 to 1999. Which other country did he earn ten caps for?**

    a) Zimbabwe

    b) Namibia

    c) Argentina

3. **Danie Rossouw, George Smith and Todd Clever have all played for which of the following sides?**

    a) Highlanders

    b) Suntory Sungoliath

    c) Saracens

4. **Which former New Zealand international was named Canada head coach in 2008?**

    a) John Kirwan

    b) Peter Sloane

    c) Kieran Crowley

5. **Who was the first Munster man to captain Ireland?**
    - a) Tom Clifford
    - b) John O'Meara
    - c) Jim McCarthy

6. **Who made his professional boxing debut with a cruiserweight win over Barry Dunnett in February 2013?**
    - a) Quade Cooper
    - b) Israel Folau
    - c) Matt Toomua

7. **England beat New Zealand 15–9 in 1983. Who bulldozed over the line to score his only international try in 25 England matches?**
    - a) Maurice Colclough
    - b) Steve Bainbridge
    - c) Paul Simpson

8. **At which stadium did Wales capture the 1971 Grand Slam with a 5–9 away victory over France?**

9. **Who broke Llanelli hearts with a last-gasp 58-metre penalty to give Leicester Tigers a 13–12 victory against the west Wales side in the semi-final of the 2002 European Cup?**

10. **Who played his last international in 2011 as Fiji's most capped player with 71 appearances and a record 670 points?**

Round 39

1. **New Zealand won the inaugural Rugby World Cup in 1987. Who captained the side to a 29–9 victory over France in the final?**

   a) David Kirk

   b) Gary Whetton

   c) Wayne Shelford

2. **How many international drop-goals were achieved in total by Hugo Porta (1971–1990), Barry John (1966–1972) and Ian McGeechan (1972–1979)?**

   a) 34

   b) 44

   c) 54

3. **The clothing brand 'Eden Park' was formed in 1987. Who was its founder?**

   a) Franck Mesnel

   b) Didier Codorniou

   c) Yves Lafarge

4. **Victor Matfield became South Africa's oldest international in 2014. Whose record did he overtake?**

   a) Johan Ackermann

   b) Boy Morkel

   c) Frik du Preez

5. **Scotland beat England in the first ever rugby international on 27 March 1871. The game was played at the Academy Ground, Raeburn Place, Edinburgh. How many players were in each side?**

   a) 13
   b) 17
   c) 20

6. **Wales defeated England 14–3 in January 1965. Who was the English scrum-half that won the last of his nine caps in the match, nine years after being awarded his eighth?**

   a) Dennis Shuttleworth
   b) Dickie Jeeps
   c) Johnny Williams

7. **Who captained the New Zealand women's team to a 25–17 win over England in the 2006 Women's Rugby World Cup final?**

   a) Emma Jensen
   b) Farah Palmer
   c) Amiria Marsh

8. **Who scored 64 tries in 101 Tests for Australia from 1982 to 1996?**

9. **Who scored 1,049 points in an 87-game career for Wales that began with his debut against England in 1991?**

10. **The book *Me and My Mouth* was released in 2006. Which Englishman's autobiography was this?**

Round 40

1. **Western Force is based in which city of Australia?**

    a) Geelong

    b) Melbourne

    c) Perth

2. **Welsh internationals Gerald Davies and Mervyn Davies shared the same first name. What was it?**

    a) Thomas

    b) Richard

    c) David

3. **Italy won their first ever Six Nations match 34–20 on 5 February 2000. Who were the opposition?**

    a) Wales

    b) Scotland

    c) France

4. **Michael Jones made 55 New Zealand Test appearances. Which country did he represent on a single occasion in 1986 prior to his All Black career?**

    a) Tonga

    b) Cook Islands

    c) Samoa

5. **Serge Blanco played his entire career for which club side?**

    a) Brive

    b) Biarritz

    c) Castres

6. **Jack Hartley won a single cap for South Africa in 1891 as a winger. What national record did he set?**

    a) Youngest international at 18 years and 18 days.
    b) First player to score four tries in a Test match.
    c) First cricket and rugby union dual international.

7. **Argentina defeated Australia 21–17 in October 2014. Who were the two try scorers for the men from South America?**

    a) Leonardo Senatore and Juan Imhoff
    b) Marcos Ayerza and Tomás Lavanini
    c) Lucas González Amorosino and Rodrigo Báez

8. **Who became the tallest man to play international rugby when a Scotland forward made his debut in 2000 standing at seven feet tall?**

9. **Gareth Edwards, Ieuan Evans and Scott Gibbs each went on three British and Irish Lions tours. Which one made the most Test appearances?**

10. **In 2010, who became the first player to be named International Rugby Board player of the year for a third time?**

Round 41

1. **Bill Dickinson became the first Scotland national coach in 1971. What was his job title?**

   a) Adviser to the captain

   b) Counsel of the president

   c) Consultant to the Scottish Rugby Union

2. **Which Irish second-row earned 51 caps for his country from 1974 to 1984?**

   a) Harold Steele

   b) Donal Spring

   c) Moss Keane

3. **All Black international brothers Graeme and Stephen Bachop played against each other twice in 1999. Who did they represent in those games?**

   a) Japan and Samoa

   b) Tonga and Fiji

   c) Italy and Georgia

4. **Wales defeated England 28–6 at Cardiff on 21 January 1922. What was noteworthy about the match?**

   a) First match broadcast by BBC radio.

   b) Last game where a conversion was worth three points.

   c) Both teams wore numbers on their jerseys in an international for the first time.

5. **Which club won the 1976 and 1977 John Player Cup?**

   a) Moseley

   b) Rosslyn Park

   c) Gosforth

6. **Sias Swart, Lofty Fourie and Jan Ellis are the only three players to have represented South Africa while playing for which side?**

   a) Border State

   b) South West Africa

   c) North East Territory

7. **Prior to Wales' game against Scotland in the 1971 Five Nations tournament, why did Clive Rowlands have to speed back to the team hotel on a police motorbike?**

   a) Gareth Edwards had forgotten his gum shield.

   b) The team shirts had been left in the hotel lobby.

   c) Denzil Williams had lost his boots.

8. **Which Australia outside-half set a 47 Test world record for a half-back combination with Nick Farr-Jones during the 1980s and 1990s?**

9. **Wayne Pivac was head coach of which national side from 2004 until 2007?**

10. **Cyril Brownlie of New Zealand in 1925 became the first person to be sent off against England. It took 55 years for the next player to be sent off against the English. Who was he?**

Round 42

1. **What colour shirt did England wear in a match against Wales in February 2010 to celebrate 100 years of international rugby at Twickenham?**
   - a) Cream
   - b) Green
   - c) Pink

2. **Who captained Scotland to the 1999 Five Nations championship?**
   - a) Stuart Grimes
   - b) Alan Tait
   - c) Gary Armstrong

3. **Mick Galway won 41 Ireland caps in an 11-year international career. How many times did his country drop him during this period?**
   - a) 9
   - b) 13
   - c) 15

4. **In 2002, which side became the first to win every match in a Super Rugby season?**
   - a) Waratahs
   - b) Crusaders
   - c) Brumbies

5. **Va'aiga Tuigamala earned 41 international caps scoring eight tries; 19 of these appearances were for New Zealand. Which other country did he play for?**

     a) Samoa

     b) Tonga

     c) Australia

6. **Diego Ormaechea scored 41 tries in 57 Test matches. Which country did he play for?**

     a) Italy

     b) Argentina

     c) Uruguay

7. **At 38 years and 198 days, which New Zealand international set the record for the oldest European Cup try scorer while playing for the Ospreys against Viadana in 2009?**

     a) Jerry Collins

     b) Filo Tiatia

     c) Marty Holah

8. **Which Australia flanker received a formal written warning by the Australian Rugby Union in 2014 for being arrested at a coalmine protest in New South Wales?**

9. **Who was the only London Welsh player on the British and Irish Lions tour of New Zealand in 1977?**

10. **Who was the only South Africa player to appear in both their 1995 and 2007 Rugby World Cup winning sides?**

Round 43

1. **How many rugby internationals lost their lives in the First World War?**
   - a) 56
   - b) 89
   - c) 111

2. **England defeated Fiji 58–23 in November 1989. Who during the game became the second Englishman to score five tries in a match?**
   - a) Mark Bailey
   - b) Jeremy Guscott
   - c) Rory Underwood

3. **Who scored four tries for Scotland against France in January 1925, then another four tries against Wales the following month?**
   - a) Ian Smith
   - b) Johnnie Wallace
   - c) Dan Drysdale

4. **Danie Gerber had a 12-year international career for South Africa following his debut against South America in 1980. How many caps did he gain?**
   - a) 12
   - b) 24
   - c) 31

5. **Who did Wales defeat 72–18 in their opening match of the 2007 Rugby World Cup?**

    a) Japan
    b) Namibia
    c) Romania

6. **Father and son, Guy and Didier Camberabero achieved which identical international record?**

    a) 36 France appearances
    b) 11 drop-goals
    c) 6 tries

7. **Who played the role of 'Frank the bookie' in the 2001 film *Very Annie Mary*?**

    a) Graham Price
    b) Ray Gravell
    c) Mark Ring

8. **Which future global superstar became the youngest Test All Black at the age of 19 years and 45 days in 1994?**

9. **Which member of Scotland's 1990 Grand Slam winning side had a New Zealand international father?**

10. **In 2009, which country won the inaugural women's Rugby World Cup Sevens competition in Dubai?**

Round 44

1. **Which emblem forms the badge on Scotland's rugby jersey?**

    a) A golden lion

    b) A thistle

    b) The Wallace Monument

2. **Which club side did Australian back Berrick Barnes join in 2013?**

    a) Canon Eagles

    b) Panasonic Wild Knights

    c) Toyota Verblitz

3. **England lost 19–12 in their quarter-final at the 2011 Rugby World Cup. Who were the victors in the match?**

    a) France

    b) Wales

    c) South Africa

4. **Who scored a brace of tries in South Africa's 37–13 Rugby World Cup semi-final win over Argentina in 2007?**

    a) JP Pietersen

    b) Fourie du Preez

    c) Bryan Habana

5. **Harlequins forward Wavell Wakefield won three Grand Slams with England in the 1920s. What did he become after retiring from rugby?**

    a) A Baptist missionary in Nigeria

    b) A Conservative Member of Parliament in the UK

    c) The Prime Minister of Jamaica

6. **Irish fly-half Jack Kyle played provincial rugby for which side?**

    a) Ulster

    b) Munster

    c) Leinster

7. **How many international tries were scored in total by David Venditti (1996–2000), Martin Leslie (1998–2003) and Simon Geoghegan (1991–1996)?**

    a) 27

    b) 33

    c) 39

8. **Who was named International Rugby Board coach of the year for a record fifth occasion in 2011?**

9. **Which two players appeared in Australia's starting line-up for both the 1991 and 1999 Rugby World Cup finals?**

10. **Which future successful businessman made the last of 40 Ireland appearances in their 32–4 loss to Wales in 1975?**

Round 45

1. **Which country became the first to achieve a third consecutive Five Nations Triple Crown with a 20–16 victory over Ireland in 1978?**

    a) Scotland

    b) Wales

    c) England

2. **Who beat New Zealand 17–12 to win Commonwealth Games Sevens gold in 2014?**

    a) Fiji

    b) Wales

    c) South Africa

3. **Australian back Matt Giteau joined which French side in 2011?**

    a) Toulon

    b) Brive

    c) Montpellier

4. **What controversial act did Tonga's Epi Taione do before the 2007 Rugby World Cup?**

    a) Requested King George V stands down due to the disparity in wealth between the royal family and the average person in Tonga.

    b) Changed his name by deed poll to Paddy Power as part of a sponsorship deal with the bookmaker.

    c) Changed allegiance to New Zealand, playing in three matches for the All Blacks.

5. **Which referee was attacked on the pitch by a South Africa fan during a 2002 international between the Springboks and All Blacks?**
   a) Joël Jutge
   b) Chris White
   c) David McHugh

6. **Who became the first British player to lift the European Cup, captaining Bath to glory in 1998?**
   a) Phil de Glanville
   b) Richard Webster
   c) Andy Nicol

7. **Which club won the 1973 and 1974 Rugby Football Union Club Knock competition, later known as the John Player Cup?**
   a) Coventry
   b) Waterloo
   c) Wasps

8. *Proud: My Autobiography* **was released in 2014. Which 100 times capped Welsh international's book was it?**

9. **Which Dutch-born winger made his debut for Scotland through the three-year residency rule in 2012?**

10. **Which All Black outside-half scored 291 points in 35 Test matches following his debut against Argentina in 1997?**

Round 46

1. **Which of the following had the highest win percentage in an Ireland shirt?**
   - a) Brian O'Driscoll
   - b) Peter Stringer
   - c) Mike Gibson

2. **Which Welshman received a red card for a tip tackle 18 minutes into Wales' 2011 Rugby World Cup semi-final match against France?**
   - a) Sam Warburton
   - b) Mike Phillips
   - c) Alun Wyn Jones

3. **Scotland used their first ever substitute in a match against France in 1969. Who was the player who took to the field that day?**
   - a) Ian McCrane
   - b) Colin Blaikie
   - c) Wilson Lauder

4. **The Antim Cup is contested between which two nations?**
   - a) USA and Canada
   - b) Italy and Spain
   - c) Georgia and Romania

5. **Who lost to a Rugby World Cup record score of 142–0 against Australia in 2003?**

    a) Portugal
    b) Namibia
    c) Spain

6. **Which club produced future England internationals Danny Grewcock, Neil Back and Tom Wood?**

    a) Walsall
    b) Berkswell and Balsall
    c) Barkers' Butts

7. **Sammy Walker, Robin Thompson and Colin Patterson were all Irish internationals. Which club did they play for?**

    a) Portadown
    b) Instonians
    c) Ballyclare

8. **South Africa defeated England 15–6 in the 2007 Rugby World Cup final. Who was the winning captain?**

9. **Why did Graham Mourie receive a ten-year ban from playing or coaching rugby?**

10. **Which country won the inaugural Rugby World Cup Sevens in 1993?**

Round 47

1. **Back-row forwards Josh Sole, Alessandro Zanni and Aaron Persico have all played international rugby. Which country have they represented?**

    a) Australia

    b) Namibia

    c) Italy

2. **Who in the 2011–12 season became the first teenager to score ten international tries?**

    a) George North

    b) Jack Nowell

    c) Jan Serfontein

3. **Who captained New Zealand to a disappointing 1999 Rugby World Cup semi-final loss to France at Twickenham?**

    a) Anton Oliver

    b) Taine Randell

    c) Byron Kelleher

4. **Tony Stanger scored a decisive try in Scotland's 13–7 victory over England in 1990, providing the home side with a third Grand Slam. Who made an under-pressure chip-kick to create the try?**

    a) Gary Armstrong

    b) Craig Chalmers

    c) Gavin Hastings

5. **Who scored 13 tries in 37 Australia appearances after a high profile switch from rugby league in 2001?**
   a) Wendell Sailor
   b) Andrew Walker
   c) Lote Tuqiri

6. **Ernest Hammett, William Hancock and Colin Smart all won England caps while playing for which Welsh club side?**
   a) Swansea
   b) Newport
   c) Pontypool

7. **Who captained the British and Irish Lions a then record six times on their 1959 tour of Australia and New Zealand?**
   a) Ronnie Dawson
   b) Andy Mulligan
   c) Bev Risman

8. **Which side became the first to win back-to-back Hong Kong Sevens Cup finals in 1977 and 1978?**

9. **England defeated South Africa 22–27 at Bloemfontein in June 2000. Who scored all the points for the visitors?**

10. **France beat New Zealand 16–3 in 1986. What happened to Wayne Shelford in the match?**

Round 48

1. **Patrick Estève, Fabien Galthié and Mathieu Bastareaud have all played international rugby. Which country have they represented?**
   a) Italy
   b) France
   c) Spain

2. **In 2003 which two Englishmen became the first players to win the Rugby World Cup in both sevens and fifteen-man versions?**
   a) Matt Dawson and Lawrence Dallaglio
   b) Josh Lewsey and Ben Cohen
   c) Mike Tindall and Neil Back

3. **Fijian-born Sitiveni Sivivatu became the first player to score four tries on a New Zealand debut. Which country was he playing against?**
   a) Wales
   b) Argentina
   c) Fiji

4. **Which English club side did Australian international Michael Lynagh join in 1996?**
   a) Bath
   b) Saracens
   c) Harlequins

5. Which of the following had a father called Jock who played in goal at football for Scotland and won the Scottish Cup with Clyde?

    a) Dougie Morgan
    b) Bruce Hay
    c) Gordon Brown

6. Schalk Burger made his South Africa debut in 2003. Which side did he play for at the time?

    a) Boland Cavaliers
    b) Western Province
    c) Golden Lions

7. On 12 July 2011, which former Wales flanker set a world record for becoming the first person to climb the highest mountain on each of the world's seven continents and stand on the North Pole, South Pole and summit of Mount Everest within a seven-month period?

    a) Richard Parks
    b) Colin Charvis
    C) Richie Collins

8. Which club won the Scottish National League Division One title for five consecutive years during the 1970s?

9. Which Canadian winger won the 2001 European Cup final with the Leicester Tigers?

10. Which Rugby World Cup winning All Black received a four-week ban for the start of the 2012 Super Rugby season after a naked, drunken rampage in the Cook Islands?

Round 49

1. **How many international points were scored in total by Jonathan Davies (1985–1997), Brendan Mullin (1984–1995) and John Eales (1991–2001)?**

   a) 326

   b) 418

   c) 523

2. **What was distinctive about Doug Howlett's appearance in New Zealand's 40–8 win over Ireland in 2002?**

   a) First All Black to score a hat-trick of tries in three consecutive games.

   b) He was the only non-Crusaders player in the side.

   c) First All Black to start a match in four different positions within the same season.

3. **England centre Manu Tuilagi was fined close to £8,000 during the 2011 Rugby World Cup. Which of the following indiscretions did he not commit?**

   a) He wore a sponsored mouth guard.

   b) He jumped off a ferry in Auckland.

   c) He trapped a hotel maid in his bedroom.

4. **Which of the following Irish outside-halves made the most British and Irish Lions Test appearances?**

   a) Ollie Campbell

   b) Ronan O'Gara

   c) Tony Ward

5. Who made 33 consecutive appearances in a Welsh jersey over a 12-year period starting with a loss to Scotland in 1890?

      a) Arthur Gould

      b) Billy Bancroft

      c) Selwyn Biggs

6. Who was the only 20th-century British and Irish Lions captain to win a series after losing the opening Test?

      a) Willie John McBride

      b) Phil Bennett

      c) Finlay Calder

7. Which country won two of the four rugby union tournaments held at the Olympic Games between 1900 and 1924?

      a) Germany

      b) France

      c) USA

8. In 1995, who told TV reporters that the Rugby Football Union committee were 'a bunch of old farts'?

9. Sanivalati Laulau set a national record of 20 tries in 32 matches when he retired in 1985. Which country did he play for?

10. Wales lost 6–9 to England at Cardiff in 1947. What did England wing Dickie Guest have in common with Wales full-back Howard Davies and scrum-half Haydn Tanner?

Round 50

1. **Who was man of the tournament at the 1991 Rugby World Cup?**
    a) Tim Horan
    b) David Campese
    c) John Eales

2. **Who set a record that stood for almost two decades for the most consecutive Tests played in an England jersey with 36 appearances from 1968 to 1975?**
    a) Keith Fairbrother
    b) David Duckham
    c) John Pullin

3. **Cardiff played Australia six times in the 20th century. How many times did they win?**
    a) Twice
    b) Four times
    c) All six games

4. **Who captained a World XV to a 14–28 victory over New Zealand at Christchurch in April 1992?**
    a) Olivier Roumat
    b) David Sole
    c) Marc Cécillon

5. **Which of the following 'near-death' experiences did not happen to Scotland international Mike Campbell-Lamerton?**

   a) Shark attack off the Florida coastline.
   b) Struck in the chest by a javelin.
   c) Standing on a mine in the Far East while on army duty.

6. **South Africa defeated Uruguay 39–3 in the pool stages of the 1999 Rugby World Cup. Whose tournament was over after being sent off for stamping in the match?**

   a) Brendan Venter
   b) Mark Andrews
   c) Cobus Visagie

7. **England defeated Australia 9–6 at Twickenham in 1958. Who scored a 60-yard try late in the game to give the home side victory?**

   a) Jim Hetherington
   b) Peter Jackson
   c) Jeff Butterfield

8. **Which Argentina back-row forward won the 2013 and 2014 European Cup with Toulon?**

9. **Who was the New Zealand outside-half that set a 45-points national record on his debut against Japan in 1995?**

10. **Who was the British and Irish Lions player to have been upended by Tana Umaga and Keven Mealamu in the first Test against New Zealand in 2005, resulting in the target dislocating his shoulder and missing the remainder of the series?**

Answers

Round 1

1. a
2. c
3. b
4. a
5. c
6. c
7. a
8. George Gregan (Australia)
9. Phil Bennett
10. Brad Thorn (2011 Rugby World Cup with New Zealand, 2008 Super Rugby with Crusaders, 2012 European Cup with Leinster).

Round 2

1. a
2. c
3. c. Against Japan.
4. c
5. b
6. a
7. a
8. Tony O'Reilly
9. Geoff Cooke
10. Scotland

Round 3

1. c
2. b
3. a
4. a
5. c
6. b
7. a
8. Ian Smith (Scotland)
9. Llanelli
10. Simon Hodgkinson

Round 4

1. c
2. a
3. b
4. c
5. a
6. b
7. a
8. Gary and Alan Whetton
9. South Africa
10. John Bentley

Round 5

1. a
2. a. Alain Penaud won 32 caps, Peter Clohessy won 54 caps and Paul Thorburn won 37.
3. c
4. c
5. b
6. a

7. b
8. Roy Laidlaw
9. André Joubert
10. Northampton

Round 6

1. b
2. a
3. c
4. a
5. c
6. c
7. b
8. Hugo Porta
9. Keith Wood
10. Errol Tobias

Round 7

1. c
2. a
3. b
4. c
5. a
6. b
7. b
8. Regan King
9. Neil Back
10. Graham Henry

Round 8

1. b
2. c

3. a
4. b
5. b
6. c
7. c
8. David Sole
9. Richie McCaw
10. Bakkies

Round 9

1. a
2. b
3. c
4. b
5. a
6. c
7. a
8. Bryan Habana
9. Grant Fox
10. JJ Williams

Round 10

1. b
2. c
3. a
4. b
5. a
6. c
7. a
8. Centre
9. Stu Wilson
10. Waisale Serevi

Round 11

1. a
2. a
3. b
4. c
5. c
6. b
7. a
8. Michael Lynagh
9. Hawick
10. England

Round 12

1. c
2. a
3. b
4. b
5. a
6. a
7. c
8. John Hipwell
9. Mike Catt
10. Clive Burgess

Round 13

1. a
2. b
3. c
4. b
5. a
6. c
7. b

8. Sandy Carmichael
9. Tom Kiernan
10. Josh Kronfeld

Round 14

1. b
2. c
3. b
4. c
5. a
6. a
7. b
8. Ireland and Italy
9. Gareth Davies and David Richards
10. Boxing

Round 15

1. c
2. a
3. c
4. a
5. b
6. c
7. a
8. Portugal
9. Andy Leslie
10. Win four Grand Slams

Round 16

1. a
2. c
3. b

4. a
5. b
6. c
7. c
8. Gavin Hastings
9. Pontypool
10. Dan Carter

Round 17

1. b
2. a
3. c
4. c
5. a
6. a
7. a. This was a record for a lock.
8. Saracens
9. Zinzan Brooke
10. Mauro and Mirco Bergamasco

Round 18

1. c
2. b
3. a
4. c
5. a
6. b
7. c
8. Tom Kiernan
9. Arthur Smith
10. Ruan Piennar

Round 19

1. c
2. b
3. a
4. c
5. b. The record stood for five years.
6. a
7. a
8. JPR Williams
9. London Irish
10. Nelson Mandela

Round 20

1. a
2. b
3. c
4. b
5. c
6. b
7. c
8. Bryan Williams
9. Toulon
10. Gareth Rees

Round 21

1. a
2. b
3. a
4. a
5. b
6. c
7. a

8. Brian O'Driscoll (133 caps for Ireland, eight caps for the British and Irish Lions).
9. Terry Price
10. Bill McLaren

Round 22

1. b
2. a
3. a
4. c
5. b
6. b
7. c
8. Bill Beaumont (The Bill Beaumont Cup).
9. Leinster
10. Tana Umaga (New Zealand) and Mike Umaga (Samoa).

Round 23

1. b
2. c
3. a
4. c
5. b
6. a
7. a
8. South Africa
9. Ryan Jones
10. Dusty Hare

Round 24

1. b
2. b
3. c
4. b. John Taylor won four caps, Jeff Squire won six caps and Derek Quinnell won five caps.
5. a
6. c
7. a
8. Limerick
9. Percy Montgomery
10. Cricket

Round 25

1. b
2. c
3. b. Piet Uys won 12 caps, Dawie de Villiers won 25 caps and Dick Lockyear won six caps.
4. a
5. c
6. a
7. b
8. Marc Lièvremont
9. Agustín Pichot
10. Andy Dalton (Andy Dalton won 35 caps, Ray Dalton won two caps).

Round 26

1. b
2. c
3. a
4. a. Malcolm O'Kelly won 92 caps, Mark Taylor won 52 caps and Olivier Roumat won 61 caps.

5. c
6. b
7. c
8. South Africa
9. Cliff Morgan
10. Didier Camberabero

Round 27

1. a
2. a
3. c
4. b
5. a
6. b
7. c
8. Sonny Bill Williams
9. Butch
10. Jean-Pierre Romeu

Round 28

1. b
2. c
3. a
4. c
5. a
6. b
7. c
8. Clermont Auvergne
9. Nick Easter
10. New Zealand

Round 29

1. b
2. c
3. a
4. b
5. c
6. c
7. a
8. Six (Five missed tackles plus a tackle two metres out but his momentum carried him across the line).
9. Argentina
10. Rex Richards

Round 30

1. b
2. a
3. a
4. b. Rosa Naas Botha
5. c
6. a
7. b
8. Australia
9. Gavin Hastings
10. Barry John

Round 31

1. b
2. c
3. a
4. c
5. a
6. c

7. b
8. John Pullin
9. John Taylor
10. Moscow

Round 32

1. a
2. a
3. b
4. c
5. c
6. c
7. a. Émile Ntamack scored 26 tries, Christophe Dominici scored 25 tries and Christian Darrouy scored 23 tries.
8. John Smit
9. Paul Ackford
10. Jeremy Davidson

Round 33

1. b
2. a
3. c
4. c
5. b. Luigi Troiani scored 57 conversions, Didier Camberabero scored 48 conversions and Arwel Thomas scored 30 conversions.
6. a
7. b
8. Gloucester
9. Eric Liddell
10. John James

Round 34

1. a
2. b
3. c. 8 tries
4. b
5. c
6. a
7. b
8. Joost van der Westhuizen
9. Dorian West
10. He drove a golf buggy while drunk on the M4 motorway looking for breakfast.

Round 35

1. c
2. b
3. b
4. a
5. b
6. c
7. b
8. Matt Burke
9. Blackheath
10. Gavin Henson

Round 36

1. b
2. a
3. b. Thomas Castaignède scored 247 points, Gérald Merceron scored 267 points and Jean-Baptiste Élissalde scored 214 points.

4. a. Scott Hastings won 65 caps, Jim Renwick won 52 caps and Tom Smith won 61 caps.
5. c
6. c
7. b
8. Crusaders
9. Stephen Jones
10. Jeff Butterfield

Round 37

1. b
2. c
3. b
4. c
5. c
6. b
7. b
8. Sébastien Chabal
9. Mark Ella
10. Ben Edwards

Round 38

1. b
2. a
3. b
4. c
5. c
6. a
7. a
8. Stade de Colombes
9. Tim Stimpson
10. Nicky Little

Round 39

1. a
2. b. Hugo Porta scored 26 drop-goals, Barry John scored ten drop-goals (including two for the British and Irish Lions) and Ian McGeechan scored eight drop-goals (including one for the British and Irish Lions).
3. a
4. a
5. c
6. c
7. b
8. David Campese
9. Neil Jenkins
10. Austin Healey

Round 40

1. c
2. a
3. b
4. c
5. b
6. a
7. a
8. Richard Metcalfe
9. Gareth Edwards. Gareth Edwards made ten appearances, Ieuan Evans made seven appearances and Scott Gibbs made five appearances.
10. Richie McCaw

Round 41

1. a
2. c

3. a. Graeme Bachop for Japan, Stephen Bachop for Samoa.
4. c
5. c
6. b
7. a
8. Michael Lynagh
9. Fiji
10. Paul Ringer (Wales)

Round 42

1. a
2. c
3. c
4. b
5. a
6. c
7. b
8. David Pocock
9. Alun Lewis
10. Os du Randt

Round 43

1. c
2. c
3. a
4. b
5. a
6. b
7. b
8. Jonah Lomu
9. Sean Lineen, his father was Terry Lineen.
10. Australia

Round 44

1. b
2. b
3. a
4. c
5. b
6. a
7. a. David Venditti scored six tries, Martin Leslie scored ten tries and Simon Geoghegan scored 11 tries.
8. Graham Henry
9. Tim Horan and John Eales.
10. Ray McLoughlin

Round 45

1. b
2. c
3. a
4. b
5. c
6. c
7. a
8. Gareth Thomas
9. Tim Visser
10. Carlos Spencer

Round 46

1. b. Brian O'Driscoll had a 61% win rate, Peter Stringer had a 69% win rate and Mike Gibson had a 49% win rate.
2. a
3. a
4. c
5. b

6. c
7. b
8. John Smit
9. He accepted royalties from his 1982 autobiography. This was classified as an act of professionalism.
10. England

Round 47

1. c
2. a
3. b
4. c
5. a
6. b
7. a. This wasn't equalled for over 40 years.
8. Fiji
9. Jonny Wilkinson
10. He lost four teeth and ripped his scrotum that he then had the physio stitch up so that he could return to the field. He then had a blow to the head that forced him off with concussion.

Round 48

1. b
2. a
3. c
4. b
5. c
6. b
7. a
8. Hawick
9. Winston Stanley
10. Zac Guildford

Round 49

1. a. Jonathan Davies scored 81 points, Brendan Mullin scored 72 points and John Eales scored 173 points.
2. b
3. c
4. a. Ollie Campbell made seven appearances, Ronan O'Gara made two appearances and Tony Ward made a single appearance.
5. b
6. c
7. c
8. Will Carling
9. Fiji
10. They were the only capped players in the teams due to the hiatus caused by the Second World War.

Round 50

1. b
2. c
3. c
4. b
5. a
6. a
7. b
8. Juan Martín Fernández Lobbe
9. Simon Culhane
10. Brian O'Driscoll